FAULT LINE OF MODERN FINANCE

QUANTITATIVE ANALYSIS BY ARTIFICIAL INTELLIGENCE

Speed of money increases with artificial intelligence. *(Lakshmi chanchal hai)*

The dream of duplicating human intelligence may be as old as humanity itself.

'We want to ask a computer, "Tell me about the merger of corporation X and corporation Y'

Table of Contents

CHAPTER 1
ARTIFICIAL INTELLIGENCE TIMELINE

Today IoT makes every electronic or electrical thing intelligent.

1950 :	Turing test launched by Alan Turing for recognising machine intelligence.
1956:	Term "Artificial Intelligence" coined.
1958:	LISP, AI programming language launched.
1964:	Computers solved Algebra word problems.
1965:	ELIZA, interactive program launched. Computers talked in English.
1997:	IBM computer, Deep Blue beats world champion Garry Kasparov in Chess.
1999:	Sony's AIBO robot dog understands 100 voice commands, learns and matures.
2001:	Spielberg's movie Artificial Intelligence nominated for 2 Oscars.
2006:	Carnegie Mellon opens Machine Learning Department
2016:	Alpha Go, Google DeepMind's AI-driven computer, won its five-match series against Lee Sedol, the reigning world champion in Go, the ancient Asian board game.

In 1927 there was only Mercedes S class, today you have 100 odd options to choose from. Options are made using speed of design to market concept using artificial intelligence in Manufacturing with big M.

CHAPTER 2
INTRODUCTION

Artificial neural network is a form of artificial intelligence which attempt to mimic the behavior of the human brain and nervous system.

ANN is composed of an input layer, hidden layers or no hidden layer and an output layer. Each layer includes neurons which are connected to all the neurons of a successive layer. Developments from artificial intelligence like artificial neural networks, ANN, can be regarded as an engineering procedure emulating the human brain activity.

Applications of ANN to atomic and nuclear physics has increased during the last two decades mainly in problems related to nuclear reactors. There are several applications of ANN in nuclear spectroscopy e.g.: alpha spectroscopy, peak to background ratio and resolution improvement of detectors employing pulse-shape treatment. ANN has been applied also in gamma-ray spectrometry for automatic identification of radionuclides

Artificial intelligence, a computerized mechanism for completing a task that feeds information and results back to itself in order to continue to improve its abilities at completing that task, is an open frontier in many industries. While the possibilities for artificial intelligence seem to be limitless, at the same time it is difficult for programmers to determine ideal ways in which to utilize these technologies and tools. This is the case for hedge fund managers as much as it is for makers of smartphones and other accessories. When considering whether to utilize artificial intelligence for investment purposes, hedge funds must consider to what extent and for what specific purpose those AI protocols will be used. In some cases, managers may opt to set up separate AIs based on different models and perspectives, each designed to collect and analyze data; by mixing and comparing a variety of these results, these AIs may be able to gain a wider view of the economic world and, therefore, make more successful investment decisions. Questions of how to set up these programs and where to focus them persist.

CHAPTER 3
FUNDS ACROSS THE INDUSTRY MAKE USE OF AI

With a growing number of hedge funds founded on principles of AI investments, it's no surprise that other, established funds are also increasingly turning toward AI as well. Some of the biggest managers in the industry have expressed interest in exploring the possibilities of AI investment strategies.

AI-based strategies are not to be confused with automation in the hedge fund industry. Whereas automation sets up a series of protocols by which machines execute trades, thereby removing the possibility of human error and emotional involvement, it does not provide machines with the capability of making investment decisions separate from human controllers. In this way, AI-based funds are exploring new territory for investors around the world. As technologies continue to improve, the finance industry will be watching to see if returns climb to match.

CHAPTER 4
ARTIFICIAL
INTELLIGENCE
ECONOMY

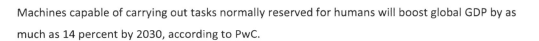

Machines capable of carrying out tasks normally reserved for humans will boost global GDP by as much as 14 percent by 2030, according to PwC.

The global auditing and consulting firm argued that the widespread adoption of artificial intelligence (AI) can contribute $15.7 trillion to the world economy over the next decade, the equivalent of the current combined output of China and India, as it would vastly increase productivity and spur shoppers to spend more.

According to the firm's calculations, the bulk of these gains, $9.1 trillion, will be generated by consumption-side effects. Shoppers, driven to work by autonomous cars, are expected to use their extra time and resources to buy personalized and higher-quality goods. The U.S. is forecast to be a major beneficiary of this trend — PwC reckons that consumption patterns triggered by AI will add $3.7 trillion to the North American economy.

CHAPTER 5
FAULT LINE

No, I am not going to talk about Prof Raghuram Rajan and his fault line fundamentals. But for those rare breeds who are new to the concept of Prof Raghu…..

Fault Lines: How Hidden Fractures Still Threaten the World Economy

Prof Rajan wrote a book on Fault Lines in 2010 to let us understand and appreciate the hidden fractures of financial crisis post 2008 which is still threatening the world economy as the name itself suggests.

At the Federal Reserve annual Jackson Hole conference in 2005, Rajan had warned about the growing risks in the financial system and proposed policies that would reduce such risks. Now the left has figured out who to blame for the financial crisis: Greedy Wall Street bankers, especially at Goldman Sachs. The right has figured it out, too: It was government's fault, especially Fannie Mae and Freddie Mac.

Raghuram Rajan of the University of Chicago's Booth School of Business says it's more complicated: Fault lines along the tectonic plates of the global economy pushed big government and big finance to a financial earthquake.

One lesson from the crisis: When nine of 10 experts say everything is fine, the audience should devote more than 10% of its time to those who say it isn't fine.

The first Rajan fault line lies in the U.S. As incomes at the top soared, politicians responded to middle-class angst about stagnant wages and insecurity over jobs and health insurance. Since they couldn't easily raise incomes—Mr. Rajan is in the camp that sees better education as the only cure and that takes time—politicians of both parties gave constituents more to spend by fostering an explosion of credit, especially for housing.

This has happened before: Farmers' grievances led to a U.S. government-backed expansion of bank credit in the 1920s; India's state-owned banks pump credit into poor constituencies in election years. But one thing was different: "When easy money pushed by a deep pocketed government comes into contact with the profit motive of a sophisticated, amoral financial sector, a deep fault line develops," Mr. Rajan writes. House prices shot up, banks borrowed cheaply and heavily to build leveraged mountains of ever more risky mortgage-linked securities.

The second fault line lies in the relentless exporting of many countries. Germany and Japan grew rich by exporting. They built agile export sectors that compete with the world's best, but shielded or strangled domestic industries such as banking and retailing. These industries are uncompetitive and inefficient, and charge high prices that discourage consumer spending.

China and others got to a similar place by a different route. Financial crises in the 1990s showed them the dangers of relying on money flowing from rich countries through local banks to finance factories, office towers and other investment. So they switched strategies, borrowed less and turned to exporting more to fuel growth. This led them to hold down exchange rates (that makes exports more attractive to others). So doing meant building huge rainy day funds of U.S. dollars.

The result: A lot of money abroad looking for a place to go met a lot of demand for borrowing in U.S. A lot of foolish loans were made.

A third Rajan fault line spread the crisis. The U.S. approach to recession-fighting—unemployment insurance and the like—and its social safety net are geared for fast, quick recoveries of the past, not for jobless recoveries now the norm. That puts pressure on Washington to do something: tax cuts, spending increases and very low interest rates. This leads big finance to assume, consciously or unconsciously, that the government will keep the money flowing and will step in if catastrophe occurs.

Compounded by hubris, envy, greed, short-sighted compensation schemes and follow-the-herd habits, these expectations that the government will save us all leads big finance to borrow cheaply and take ever bigger risks. No democratic government can let ordinary folk suffer when the harshness of the market brings the party to an end, as it inevitable does. Big finance exploits what Mr. Rajan calls this "government decency" and bets accordingly.

If he's right, changing the rules, incentives and innards of major economies to reduce the risks of repeating the recent crisis is not going to be easy.

CHAPTER 6 Tracing the financial future from the crisis point

The financial collapse of 2007 and the Great Recession that followed left many economists to rethink and debate about the issue. Why didn't we see it coming? What happened to the usual regulatory checks and balances? What happened to the discipline imposed by markets? What happened to the private instinct for self-preservation? Is the free enterprise system fundamentally flawed? Why was the flood of money that came in from outside the United States used for financing subprime credit? Why was the United States, like any other economies such as Germany and Japan, unable to export its way out of 2001 recession? Why are poorer developing countries like the China financing and unsustainable consumption of rich countries like United States? Why did the Federal Reserve keep rates so low for so long?

As the world economy tiptoes back from the precipice, there is a growing appetite for books that try to read the future. Two thoughtful studies—one by a former Economist journalist and commentator on globalisation, Philippe Legrain, and the other by Raghuram Rajan, once the chief economist at the IMF and now at the University of Chicago—aim at giving readers a deeper understanding of the forces that brought about the worst financial and economic crisis in at least half a century and look at what can be done to prevent the next one.

Mr Legrain outlines the forces that brought the world to the brink of a bust: a house-price bubble boosted by runaway mortgage lending in the rich world, particularly America, a lightly regulated global financial system that found ever-more creative ways to speculate on rising house prices, and macroeconomic policymaking that was far too laid back about the dangers posed by asset-price bubbles. None of this is new. But Mr Legrain has a gift for combining big numbers that offer a sense of the scale of the global build-up in things like household debt while zeroing in on what all this means for people like Thorvaldur Thorvaldsson, a proudly left-wing Icelandic carpenter and unlikely sometime property speculator. This makes his book a particularly good survey of what made up the unpleasant cocktail which the world has yet to digest.

But what led to this massive expansion of easy credit to the less than credit- worthy? Mr Rajan's answer, economic inequality, will surprise many. He argues provocatively that successive American governments chose cheap credit as a sop to the less-skilled parts of its workforce, who increasingly felt themselves being left behind in a globalised world. Along with all the proposals to regulate finance and find ways to allow banks to fail without bringing the rest of the economy down with them, Mr Rajan argues, America would do well to take a hard look at how it educates its young and what safety net it provides to its poor. Expanding access to education may seem like an unusual step to stress when advising governments how to avoid another financial crisis, but Mr Rajan has taken such controversial stances before. In 2005, he shocked bankers at a celebration honouring Alan Greenspan, who was about to retire as chairman of the Federal Reserve, with a paper that argued, unusually then, that financial innovation had made the world economy less safe.

Both books say it would be folly to eliminate the benefits of a more open, globalised world—including vastly improved standards of living for millions in the emerging world—because of disgust with the depredations of the financial sector. Mr Legrain cites innovative, entrepreneurial and peripatetic Swedes and Indians to drive home his central thesis that both rich and emerging countries stand to gain from the latter's increasing economic dynamism. In particular, he makes a strong pitch for the freer movement of people across borders. Both authors would also like institutions like the IMF to be reformed in such a way that would allow them to play a greater role in sorting out the macroeconomic imbalances that underlay the crisis.

Mr Rajan, however, was the fund's chief economist when it tried, with little success, to get a serious conversation going on this matter. For that reason, perhaps, his book, excellent though it is, has less of a "can do" feeling about it than Mr Legrain's. Despite that, both deserve to be widely read in a time when the tendency to blame everything on catch-all terms like "globalisation" is gaining ground.

CHAPTER 7
Quantitative Analysis in Investment Banking

While finance seeks to meet the needs of today's globalized modern economies, it must also face a considerable increase in risk. In order to conduct activities in this complex and changing environment, investment banks, hedge funds and private equity firms are always on the lookout for professionals able to identify profitable investment opportunities and manage risk. Quantitative analysts have the necessary skillset to do so.

Demand for quantitative analysts has grown...

The financial sector is characterized by constant change and innovation. Over the past few years, securities have become more and more complex. Specialists who are able to understand the mathematical models behind security pricings to generate profits and reduce risks are highly valued in the market. The growth of hedge funds and automated trading systems is another trend that has positively impacted on demand for quants.

And demand will certainly continue to grow

The 2008 crisis exposed some of the limitations of financial systems. To reduce risk and prevent future crises, policy-makers have implemented financial reforms. Regulatory authorities are now requiring unprecedented risk transparency reporting, and investors are demanding better risk infrastructures to protect their investments. Since the crisis, the risk management industry has been experiencing dramatic growth and it will continue to grow to meet increased regulatory standards. This represents a real opportunity for quants wishing to pursue a career in this field of expertise.

Quantitative analyst jobs are highly stimulating...

Having a career as a quantitative analyst is intellectually challenging, as an important part of your role is to solve complex problems while under pressure. Working in quantitative analysis involves research, the development and implementation of mathematical models, data analysis, general financial knowledge, and many other elements that make this job very stimulating. You need to be able to thrive in an environment with little supervision and under considerable pressure. Quantitative analyst jobs are highly competitive and demanding, the hours are long – but unlike many other jobs, success in this field is based on merit, dedication and knowledge rather than networking or politics.

And this career path is financially rewarding too

Quantitative analyst jobs are rewarding both intellectually and financially. Salaries in the financial sector tend to be very high. Due to the challenging nature of the work and the skills required to succeed in this kind of position, quantitative analysts are generally very well compensated, especially if they work for a hedge fund. Moreover, quantitative analyst jobs are mostly found in major financial centers such as New York, Hong Kong, London and Paris, where average salaries are higher than in secondary cities. For example, the average pay for a quantitative analyst is £61,828 per year in London (England) and $102,000 in New York (US).

CHAPTER 8
Artificial
Intelligence

Artificial intelligence, commonly abbreviated as AI, also known as machine intelligence, may be defined as "making a machine behave in ways that would be called intelligent if a human were so behaving". (This definition was put forth by John McCarthy in his 1955 Proposal for the Dartmouth Summer Research Project On Artificial Intelligence.)

The term artificial intelligence (AI) refers to a set of computer science techniques that enable systems to perform tasks normally requiring human intelligence, such as visual perception, speech recognition, decision-making and language translation. Machine learning and deep learning are branches of AI which, based on algorithms and powerful data analysis, enable computers to learn and adapt independently. For ease of reference we will use "artificial intelligence", or AI, throughout this report to refer to machine learning, deep learning and other related techniques and technologies.

Since that time several distinct types of artificial intelligence have been elucidated:

Strong artificial intelligence deals with the creation of some form of computer-based artificial intelligence that can truly reason and solve problems; a strong form of AI is said to be sentient, or self-aware. In theory, there are two types of strong AI:

Human-like AI, in which the computer program thinks and reasons much like a human mind.

Non-human-like AI, in which the computer program develops a totally non-human sentience, and a non-human way of thinking and reasoning.

Weak artificial intelligence deals with the creation of some form of computer-based artificial intelligence that cannot truly reason and solve problems; such a machine would, in some ways, act as if it were intelligent, but it would not possesses true intelligence or sentience.

To date, much of the work in this field has been done with computer simulations of intelligence based on predefined sets of rules. Very little progress has been made in strong AI. Depending on how one defines one's goals, a moderate amount of progress has been made in weak AI.

Examples

Some of the A I examples around us are :

LEGO Sudoku Bot: Are computers or humans better at Sudoku?

Pancake Bot: Are computers better at making pancakes?

Robot Dog: Are computers better at moving about?

Robot Arm: Better at catching a something?

Google Self-Driving Cars: And what about driving? (Note: the idea of "self-driving" relies heavily on what the experience of driving is like, which is non-trivially different if you are teaching in India versus Peru.)

CHAPTER 9
Development of AI theory

Much of the (original) focus of artificial intelligence research draws from an experimental approach to psychology, and emphasizes what may be called linguistic intelligence (best exemplified in the Turing test).

Approaches to artificial intelligence that do not focus on linguistic intelligence include robotics and collective intelligence approaches, which focus on active manipulation of an environment, or consensus decision making, and draw from biology and political science when seeking models of how "intelligent" behaviour is organized.

Artificial intelligence theory also draws from animal studies, in particular with insects, which are easier to emulate as robots (see artificial life), or with apes, who resemble humans in many ways but have less developed capacities for planning and cognition. AI researchers argue that animals which are simpler than humans ought to be considerably easier to mimic.

Seminal papers advancing the concept of machine intelligence include A Logical Calculus of the Ideas Immanent in Nervous Activity (1943), by Warren McCulloch and Walter Pitts, and On Computing Machinery and Intelligence (1950), by Alan Turing, and Man-Computer Symbiosis by J.C.R. Licklider. See cybernetics and Turing test for further discussion.

There were also early papers which denied the possibility of machine intelligence on logical or philosophical grounds such as Minds, Machines and Gödel (1961) by John Lucas.

With the development of practical techniques based on AI research, advocates of AI have argued that opponents of AI have repeatedly changed their position on tasks such as computer chess or speech recognition that were previously regarded as "intelligent" in order to deny the accomplishments of AI. They point out that this moving of the goalposts effectively defines "intelligence" as "whatever humans can do that machines cannot".

John von Neumann (quoted by E.T. Jaynes) anticipated this in 1948 by saying, in response to a comment at a lecture that it was impossible for a machine to think: "You insist that there is something a machine cannot do. If you will tell me precisely what it is that a machine cannot do, then I can always make a machine which will do just that!". Von Neumann was presumably alluding to the Church-Turing thesis which states that any effective procedure can be simulated by a (generalized) computer.

1969 McCarthy and Hayes started the discussion about the frame problem with their essay, "Some Philosophical Problems from the Standpoint of Artificial Intelligence".

CHAPTER 10
Experimental AI research

Artificial intelligence began as an experimental field in the 1950s with such pioneers as Allen Newell and Herbert Simon, who founded the first artificial intelligence laboratory at Carnegie-Mellon University, and McCarthy and Minsky, who founded the MIT AI Lab in 1959. They all attended the aforementioned Dartmouth College summer AI conference in 1956, which was organized by McCarthy, Minsky, and Nathan Rochester of IBM.

Historically, there are two broad styles of AI research - the "neats" and "scruffies". "Neat", classical or symbolic AI research, in general, involves symbolic manipulation of abstract concepts, and is the methodology used in most expert systems. Parallel to this are the "scruffy", or "connectionist", approaches, of which neural networks are the best-known example, which try to "evolve" intelligence through building systems and then improving them through some automatic process rather than systematically designing something to complete the task. Both approaches appeared very early in AI history. Throughout the 1960s and 1970s scruffy approaches were pushed to the background, but interest was regained in the 1980s when the limitations of the "neat" approaches of the time became clearer. However, it has become clear that contemporary methods using both broad approaches have severe limitations.

CHAPTER 11
Practical applications of AI techniques

Whilst progress towards the ultimate goal of human-like intelligence has been slow, many spinoffs have come in the process. Notable examples include the languages LISP and Prolog, which were invented for AI research but are now used for non-AI tasks. Hacker culture first sprang from AI laboratories, in particular the MIT AI Lab, home at various times to such luminaries as McCarthy, Minsky, Seymour Papert (who developed Logo there), Terry Winograd (who abandoned AI after developing SHRDLU).

- Many other useful systems have been built using technologies that at least once were active areas of AI research. Some examples include:

- Deep Blue, a chess-playing computer, beat Garry Kasparov in a famous match in 1997.

- Fuzzy logic, a technique for reasoning under uncertainty, has been widely used in industrial control systems.

- Expert systems are being used to some extent industrially.

- Machine translation systems such as SYSTRAN are widely used, although results are not yet comparable with human translators.

- Neural networks have been used for a wide variety of tasks, from intrusion detection systems to computer games.

- Optical character recognition systems can translate arbitrary typewritten European script into text.

- Handwriting recognition is used in millions of personal digital assistants.

- Speech recognition is commercially available and is widely deployed.

- Computer algebra systems, such as Mathematica and Macsyma[?], are commonplace.

- Machine vision systems are used in many industrial applications.

The vision of artificial intelligence replacing human professional judgment has arisen many times in the history of the field, and today in some specialized areas where "expert systems" are used to augment or to replace professional judgment in some areas of engineering and of medicine.

CHAPTER 12
Hypothetical consequences of AI

Some observers foresee the development of systems that are far more intelligent and complex than anything currently known. One name for these hypothetical systems is **artilects.**

With the introduction of artificially intelligent non-deterministic systems, many ethical issues will arise. Many of these issues have never been encountered by humanity.

Over time, debates have tended to focus less and less on "possibility" and more on "desirability", as emphasized in the "Cosmist" (versus "Terran") debates initiated by Hugo De Garis and Kevin Warwick. A Cosmist, according to de Garis, is actually seeking to build more intelligent successors to the human species. The emergence of this debate suggests that desirability questions may also have influenced some of the early thinkers "against".

Some issues that bring up interesting ethical questions are:

Determining the sentience of a system we create.

Turing test

Cognition

Why do we have a need to categorize these systems at all

Freedoms and rights for these systems.

Designing systems that are far more impressive than any one human

Deciding how much safe-guards to design into these systems

Seeing how much learning capability a system needs to replicate human thought, or how well it could do tasks without it (eg expert system)

The Singularity

CHAPTER 13 CAN COMPUTERS EVER BECOME AS SMART AS HUMANS?

"I believe there is no deep difference between what can be achieved by a biological brain and what can be achieved by a computer. It therefore follows that computers can, in theory, emulate human intelligence — and exceed it." - Stephen Hawking

Self-driving cars offer a good example of the amount of work that needs to go in before AI systems can reach human level intelligence. Because there are things that humans understand when approaching certain situations that would be difficult to teach to a machine. In a long blog post on autonomous cars, Rodney Brooks brings up a number of such situations, including how an autonomous car might approach a stop sign at a cross walk in a city neighborhood with an adult and child standing at the corner chatting. The algorithm would probably be tuned to wait for the pedestrians to cross, but what if they had no intention of crossing because they were waiting for a school bus? A human driver could signal to the pedestrians to go, and they in turn could wave the car on, but a driverless car could potentially be stuck there endlessly waiting for the pair to cross because they have no understanding of these uniquely human signals.

But one thing is certain. Given the recent developments in the field of AI, there will come a day when humans will not be the smartest entity on this planet. What happens then? Will computers annihilate humans or continue to serve them? And how can we put safeguards in place?

One option is to find market solutions, putting up money to fund research in ethical and safe AI, as Musk has done with OpenAI. The other is more dangerous. At a gathering of US governors earlier this month, Musk pressed them to "be proactive about regulation". What precisely does that entail? Pure research and their practical applications interact constantly to push the field of AI and robotics forward. Government control and red tape to stave off a vague, imprecise threat would be an innovation-killer.

"The rise of powerful AI will be either the best, or the worst thing, ever to happen to humanity. We do not yet know which."

— Stephen Hawking

CHAPTER 14 QUANTITATIVE ANALYSIS BY ARTIFICIAL INTELLIGENCE

Artificial intelligence, once the stuff of sci-fi fantasies, is closing in on Wall Street. A corps of scientists is trying to teach computers to think like traders—and outsmart human stock pickers.

- Jason Kelly

Trading and stock markets have been extensively using Black-Scholes formulae to price European options which was originated from the seminal papers of Black and Scholes (1973) and Merton (1973) with focuses on the following assumptions:

1. Create risk-free portfolios through dynamic hedging so that the portfolios earn risk-free interest rate;

2. Ensure an absence of arbitrage environment (Efficient markets);

3. Ensure no commission;

4. Ensure no interest rate change; and

5. Assume that stock returns follow a lognormal distribution.

However, in the real world commissions do exit and interest rates can change. Whether markets are efficient or not is still debatable. Furthermore, volatility smile has proven that stock returns and foreign exchange markets do not follow a lognormal distribution. Since Black-Scholes formulae relies on these questionable underlying assumptions, an alternative approach should be considered. Recently, artificial intelligence technology has been applied to develop an option pricing system to adjust itself to dynamic environments with no underlying assumption.

Kearns, a computer scientist who has a doctorate from Harvard University, says the code is part of a dream he's been chasing for more **than two decades: to imbue computers with artificial intelligence,** or AI. His vision of Wall Street conjures up science fiction fantasies of HAL 9000, the sentient computer in 2001: A Space Odyssey. Instead of mindlessly crunching numbers, AI-powered circuitry one day will mimic our brains and understand our emotions—and outsmart human stock pickers.

This is going to change the world, and it's going to change Wall Street says Kearns, who spent the 1990s researching AI at Murray Hill, New Jersey–based Bell Laboratories, birthplace of the laser and the transistor.

As finance Ph.D.s, mathematicians and other computer loving disciples of quantitative analysis challenge traditional traders and money managers, Kearns and a small band of AI scientists have set out to build the ultimate money machine.

For decades, investment banks and hedge fund firms have employed quants and their computers to uncover relationships in the markets and exploit them with rapid-fire trades.

Quants seek to strip human emotions such as fear and greed out of investing. Today, their brand of computer-guided trading has reached levels undreamed of a decade ago. A third of all U.S. stock trades in 2006 were driven by automatic programs, or algorithms, according to Boston-based consulting firm Aite Group LLC. By 2010, that figure will reach 50 percent, according to Aite.

AI proponents say their time is at hand. Vasant Dhar, a former Morgan Stanley quant who teaches at New York University's Stern School of Business in Manhattan's Greenwich Village, is trying to program a computer to predict the ways in which unexpected events, such as the sudden death of an executive, might affect a company's stock price. Uptown, at Columbia University, computer science professor Kathleen Mc Keown says she imagines building an electronic Warren Buffett that would be able to answer just about any kind of investing question. "We want to be able to ask a computer, 'Tell me about the merger of corporation X and corporation Y,' or 'Tell me about the impact on the markets of sending more troops to Iraq,'" McKeown, 52, says.

Some executives and scientists would rather not talk about AI. It recalls dashed hopes of artificially intelligent machines that would build cities in space and mind the kids at home. In 2001, the novel written by Arthur C. Clarke and made into a movie directed by Stanley Kubrick in 1968, HAL, a computer that can think, talk and see, is invented in the distant future—which is 1997 in the story. Things didn't turn out as '60s cyberneticists predicted. Somewhere between science fiction and science fact, the dream fell apart. People began joking that AI stood for Almost Implemented.

"The promise has always been more than the delivery," says Brian Hamilton, chief executive officer of Raleigh, North Carolina–based software maker Sageworks Inc., which uses computer formulas to automatically read stock prices, company earnings and other data and spit out reports for investors.

Hamilton, 43, says today's AI-style programs can solve specific problems within a given set of parameters. Take chess. Deep Blue, a chess-playing supercomputer developed by International Business Machines Corp., defeated world champion Garry Kasparov in 1997. The rules of chess never change, however. Players have one goal: to capture the opponent's king. There are only so many moves a player can make, and Deep Blue could evaluate 200 million such positions a second. Financial markets, on the other hand, can be influenced by just about anything, from skirmishes in the Middle East to hurricanes in the Gulf of Mexico. In computerspeak, chess is a closed system and the market is an open one. "AI is very effective when there's a specific solution," Hamilton says.

"The real challenge is where judgment is required, and that's where AI has largely failed."

AI researchers have made progress over the years. Peek inside your Web browser or your car's cruise control, and you'll probably find AI at work. Meanwhile, computer chips keep getting more powerful. In February, Santa Clara, California–based Intel Corp. said it had devised a chip the size of a thumbnail that could perform a trillion calculations a second.

Ten years ago, such a computational feat would have required 10,000 processors.

To believers such as Dhar, Kearns and McKeown, all of this is only the beginning. One day, a subfield of AI known as machine learning, Kearns's specialty, may give computers the ability to develop their own smarts and extract rules from massive data sets. Another branch, called natural language

processing, or NLP, holds out the prospect of software that can understand human language, read up on companies, listen to executives and distill what it learns into trading programs.

Collective Intellect Inc., a Boulder, Colorado–based startup, already employs basic NLP programs to comb through 55 million Web logs and turn up information that might make money for hedge funds. "There's some nuggets of wisdom in the sea," says Collective Intellect Chief Technology Officer Tim Wolters. Another AI area, neural networking, involves building silicon versions of the cerebral cortex, the part of our brain that governs reason. The hope is that these systems will ape living neurons, think like people and, like traders, understand that some things are neither black nor white but rather in varying shades of gray.

Trust Corp. in Atlanta, says computers can mine data and see relationships that humans can't. Quantitative investing is on the rise, and that's bound to spur interest in AI, says Macey, who previously developed computer models at Marietta, Georgia–based American Financial Advisors LLC, to weigh investment risk and project clients' wealth. "It's all over the place and, greed being what it will, people will try anything to get an edge," Macey, 46, says. "Quant is everywhere, and it's seeping into everything." AI proponents are positioning themselves to become Wall Street's hyperquants. Kearns, who previously ran the quant team within the equity strategies group at Lehman Brothers, splits his time between the University of Pennsylvania in Philadelphia, where he teaches computer science, and the New York investment bank, where he tries to put theory into practice. Neither he nor Lehman executives would discuss how the firm uses computers to trade, saying the programs are proprietary and that divulging information about them would cost the firm its edge in the markets. On an overcast Monday in late January, Kearns is at work few members of his team drop by for advice. At Lehman, Kearns is the big thinker on AI. He leaves most of the actual programming to a handful of Ph.D.s, most of whom he's recruited at universities or computer conferences. Kearns himself was plucked from Penn. Ian Lowitt, who studied with Kearns at the University of Oxford and is now co-chief administrative officer of Lehman Brothers, persuaded him to come to the firm as a consultant in 2002. Kearns hardly looks the part of a professor. He has closely cropped black hair and sports a charcoal gray suit and a crisp blue shirt and tie. At Penn, his students compete to design trading strategies for the Penn-Lehman Automated Trading Project, which uses a computerized trading simulator. Tucking into a lunch of tempura and sashimi at a Japanese restaurant near Lehman Brothers, Kearns says AI's failure to live up to its sci-fi hype has created many doubters on Wall Street. He says people should be skeptical: Trading requires institutional knowledge that is difficult, if not impossible, to program into a computer. AI holds perils as well as promise for Wall Street, Kearns says. Right now, even sophisticated AI programs lack common sense, he says. "When something is going awry in the markets, people can quickly sense it and stop trading," he says. "If you have completely automated something, it might not be able to do that, and that makes you subject to catastrophic risk." The dream of duplicating human intelligence may be as old as humanity itself. The intellectual roots of AI go back to ancient myths and tales such as Ovid's story of Pygmalion, the sculptor who fell so in love with his creation that the gods brought his work to life. In the 19th century, English mathematician and proto-computer scientist Charles Babbage originated the idea of a programmable computer. It wasn't until 1951, however, that British mathematician Alan Turing proposed a test for a machine's capability for thought. In a paper titled "Computing Machinery and Intelligence," Turing, a computer pioneer who'd worked at Bletchley Park, Britain's World War II code-breaking center, suggested the following: A human judge engages in a text-only conversation with two parties, one human and the other a machine. If the judge can't reliably tell which is which, the machine passes and can be said to possess intelligence. No computer has ever done that. Turing committed suicide in 1954. Two years later, computer scientist John McCarthy coined the phrase artificial intelligence to refer to the science of engineering thinking machines. The Turing Test, as it's now known, has fueled almost six decades of controversy. Some computer scientists and philosophers say human-like interaction is essential to human-like intelligence. Others say it's not. The debate still shapes AI research and raises questions about whether traders' knowledge, creativity, intuition and appetite for risk can ever be programmed into a computer

During the 1960s and '70s, AI research yielded few commercial applications. As Wall Street firms deployed computer-driven program trading in the '80s to automatically execute orders and allow arbitrage between stocks, options and futures, the AI world began to splinter. Researchers broke away into an array of camps, each focusing on specific applications rather than on building HAL-like machines. Some scientists went off to develop computers that could mimic the human retina in its ability to see and recognize complex images such as faces. Some began applying AI to robotics. Still others set to work on programs that could read and understand human languages. Thomas Mitchell, chairman of the Machine Learning Department at Carnegie Mellon University in Pittsburgh, says many AI researchers have decided to reach for less and accomplish more. "It's really matured from saying there's one big AI label to being a little more refined and realizing there are some specific areas where we really have made progress," Mitchell, 55, says. Financial service companies have already begun to deploy basic machine-learning programs, Kearns says. Such programs typically work in reverse to solve problems and learn from mistakes. Like every move a player makes in a game of chess, every trade changes the potential outcome, he says. Machine-learning algorithms are designed to examine possible scenarios at every point along the way, from beginning to middle to end, and figure out the best choice at each moment. Kearns likens the process to learning to play chess. "You would never think about teaching a kid to play chess by playing in total silence and then saying at the end, 'You won' or 'You lost,'" he says. As an exercise, Kearns and his colleagues at Lehman Brothers used such programs to examine orders and improve how the firm executes trades, he says. The programs scanned bids, offers, specific prices and buy and sell orders to find patterns in volatility and prices, he says. Using this information, they taught a computer how to determine the most cost-effective trades. The program worked backward, assessing possible trades and enabling trader-programmers to evaluate the impact of their actions. By working this way, the computer learns how to execute trades going forward. Language represents one of the biggest gulfs between human and computer intelligence, Dhar says. Closing that divide would mean big money for Wall Street, he says. Unlike computers, human traders and money managers can glimpse a CEO on television or glance at news reports and sense whether news is good or bad for a stock. In conversation, a person's vocal tone or inflection can alter—or even reverse—the meaning of words. Let's say you ask a trader if he thinks U.S. stocks are cheap and he responds, "Yeah, right." Does he mean stocks are inexpensive or, sarcastically, just the opposite? What matters is not just what people say, but how they say it. Traders also have a feel for what other investors are thinking, so they can make educated guesses about how people will react

For Dhar, the markets are the ultimate AI lab. "Reality is the acid test," says Dhar, a 1978 graduate of the Indian Institutes of Technology, or IIT, whose campuses are India's best schools for engineering and computer science. He collected his doctorate in artificial intelligence from the University of Pittsburgh. A professor of information systems at Stern, Dhar left the school to become a principal at Morgan Stanley from 1994 to '97, where he founded the data-mining group and focused on automated trading and the profiling of asset management clients. He still builds computer models to help Wall Street firms predict markets and figure out clients' needs. Since 2002, his models have correctly predicted the stock prices from month to month 61 percent of the time, he says. Dhar says AI programs typically start with a human hunch about the markets. Let's say you think that rising volatility in stock prices may signal a coming "breakout," Wall Street–speak for an abrupt rise or fall in prices. Dhar says he would select market indicators for volatility and stock prices, feed them into his AI algorithms and let them check whether that intuition is right. If it is, the program would look for market patterns that hold up over time and base trades on them. Surrounded by stacks of papers and books in his Greenwich Village office, Dhar, wearing jeans and a black V-neck sweater, says many AI scientists are questing after NLP programs that can understand human language. "That's the next frontier," he says. At Columbia, McKeown leads a team of researchers trying to make sense of all the words on the Internet. When she arrived at the university 25 years ago, NLP was still in its infancy. Now, the Internet has revolutionized the field, she says. Just about anyone with a computer can access news reports, blogs and chat rooms in languages from all over the world. Rather than flowing sequentially, from point A to point B, information moves around the Web haphazardly. So, instead of creating sequential rules to instruct computers to read the information, AI specialists create an array of rules and try to enable computers to figure out what works. McKeown, who earned her doctorate from Penn, has spent the past 10 years developing a program called NewsBlaster, which collects and sorts news and information from the Web and draws conclusions from it. Sitting in her seventh-floor office in a building that's tucked behind Columbia's Low Library, McKeown describes how NewsBlaster crawls the Web each night to produce summaries on topics from politics to finance. She decided to put the system on line after the terrorist attacks of Sept. 11, 2001, to monitor the unfolding story NewsBlaster, which isn't available for commercial use, can "read" two news stories on the same topic, highlight the differences and describe what's changed since it last scanned a report on the subject, McKeown says. The program can be applied to market-moving topics such as corporate takeovers and interest rates, she says. McKeown is trying to upgrade her program so it can answer broad "what-if " questions, such as, "What if there's an earthquake in Indonesia?" Her hope is that one day, perhaps within a few years, the program will be able to write a few paragraphs or pages of answers to such open-ended questions. Dhar says computer scientists eventually will stitch together advances in machine learning and NLP and set the combined programs loose on the markets. A crucial step will be figuring out the types of data AI programs should employ. The old programmer principle of GIGO—garbage in, garbage out— still applies. If you tell a computer to look for relationships between, say, solar flares and the Dow industrials and base trades on the patterns, the computer will do it. You might not make much money, however. "If I give an NLP algorithm ore, it might give me gold," Dhar says. "If I give it garbage, it'll give me back garbage." Collective Intellect, financed by Denverbased venture capital firm Appian Ventures Inc., is trying to sell hedge funds and investment banks on NLP technology. Wolters says traders and money managers simply can't stay on top of all the information flooding the markets these days. Collective Intellect seeds its NLP programs with the names of authors, Web sites and blogs that its programmers think might yield moneymaking information. Then, the company lets the programs search the Web, make connections and come up with lists of sources they can monitor and update. Collective Intellect is pitching the idea to hedge funds, Wolters says. Technology has upended the financial services industry before. Just think of automated teller machines. Michael Thiemann, CEO of San Diego–based hedge fund firm Investment Science Corp., likens traditional Wall Street traders to personal loan officers at U.S. banks back in the '80s. Many of these loan officers lost their jobs when banks began assigning scores to customers based on a statistical analysis of their credit histories. In the U.S., those are known as FICO scores, after Minneapolis-based Fair Isaac Corp., which developed them. Computers often did a better job of assessing risk than human loan officers, Thiemann, 50, says. "And that is where

Wall Street is going," he says. Human traders will still provide insights into the markets, he says; more and more, however, those insights will be based on data rather than intuition. Thiemann, who has a master's degree in engineering from Stanford University and an MBA from Harvard Business School, knows algorithms. During the '90s, he helped HNC Software Inc., now part of Fair Isaac, develop a tracking program called Falcon to spot credit card fraud.

Falcon, which today watches over more than 450 million credit and debit cards, uses computer models to evaluate the likelihood that transactions are bogus. It weighs that risk against customers' value to the credit card issuer and suggests whether to let the charges go through or terminate them. "If it's a customer with a questionable transaction and you don't mind losing them as a customer, you just deny it," Thiemann says. "If it's a great customer and a small transaction, you let it go through, but maybe follow up with a call a day or so later." Thiemann says he's taking a similar approach with a trading system he's building. He calls his program Deep Green. The name recalls IBM's Deep Blue—and money. His program evaluates market data, learns from it and scores trading strategies for stocks, options and other investments, he says. Thiemann declines to discuss his computerized hedge fund, beyond saying that he's currently investing money for friends and family and that he plans to seek other investors this year. "This is hard, like a moon launch is hard," Thiemann says of the task ahead of him. As AI invades Wall Street, even the quants will have to change with the times. The kind of conventional trading programs that hunt out arbitrage opportunities between stocks, options and futures, for example, amount to brute-force computing. Such programs, much like Deep Blue, merely crunch a lot of numbers quickly. "They just have to be fast and comprehensive," Thiemann says. AI systems, by contrast, are designed to adapt and learn as they go. Dhar says he doubts thinking computers will displace human traders anytime soon. Instead, the machines and their creators will learn to work together. "This doesn't get rid of the rule of human creativity; it actually makes it more important," he says. "You have to be in tune with the market and be able to say, 'I'm smelling something here that's worth learning about.'" At Collective Intellect, Vice President Darren Kelly, a former BMO Nesbitt Burns Inc. stock analyst, says tomorrow's quants will rely on AI to spot patterns that no one has imagined in the free-flowing type of information that can be found in e-mails, on Web pages and in voice recordings. After all, such unstructured information accounts for about 80 percent of all the info out there. "The next generation of quant may be around unstructured analytics," Kelly says. After more than 50 years, the quest for human-level artificial intelligence has yet to yield its HAL 9000. Kearns says he'd settle for making AI pay off on Wall Street. "We're building systems that can wade out in the human world and understand it," Kearns says. Traders may never shoot the breeze with a computer at the bar after work. But the machines just might help them pay the bill.

CHAPTER 15
CONCLUSION

Quantitative Investing, one of the latest paths available to hedge fund managers and incorporating computer analytics in innovative new ways in order to make precision investment decisions, may have a new challenger emerging from within its own ranks. According to a recent report, the quickly-changing landscape of alternative investing strategies has seen a sudden rise in the prominence of artificial intelligence-based (AI) funds, and that many of these funds are vastly outperforming so-called "traditional quants", as well as human-led management teams.

Over 60 per cent of marketers in India believe new-age technologies are going to impact their workplace practices and consider it the next big disruptor in the industry.

The hedge fund industry seems to be turning toward artificially intelligent investing programs in favor of human traders in growing proportions. At a time in which artificial intelligence is sweeping the technological world, with "smart" features appearing in new accessories and appliances every month, some may have expected that it was only a matter of time before the financial world would incorporate programs and algorithms specifically designed for investment purposes. This is not to say, though, that human involvement is out and that machines will be running the hedge fund world in the immediate future. There are still many important factors and decisions that have been left to the human operators, at least for now.

BIBLIOGRAPHY

Fascinated by the modern concepts of finance and my innate passion for mathematics , I kept reading and collecting nuances from the following sources for my own understanding but then thought to share with my small world of friends, peers and audience:

- The Economist

- The Economic Times

- Raghuram Rajan's lectures and books

- Subrahmanyam Swami speeches– for contrasting views as 360 degree evaluation

- Lectures of IIM Calcutta by Prof BBC , Prof AB and Prof Anindya Sen

- Bloomberg

- Time

- Ivy League Blogs

- PwC

COVER PAGE

The dream of duplicating human intelligence may be as old as humanity itself. 'We want to ask a computer, "Tell me about the merger of corporation X and corporation Y'

No, I am not going to talk about Prof Raghuram Rajan and his fault line fundamentals. But for those rare breeds who are new to the concept of Prof Raghu..... Prof Rajan wrote a book on Fault Lines in 2010 to let us understand and appreciate the hidden fractures of financial crisis post 2008 which is still threatening the world economy as the name itself suggests.

At the Federal Reserve annual Jackson Hole conference in 2005, Rajan had warned about the growing risks in the financial system and proposed policies that would reduce such risks. Now the left has figured out who to blame for the financial crisis: Greedy Wall Street bankers, especially at Goldman Sachs. The right has figured it out, too: It was government's fault, especially Fannie Mae and Freddie Mac.

Quantitative investing, one of the latest paths available to hedge fund managers and incorporating computer analytics in innovative new ways in order to make precision investment decisions, may have a new challenger emerging from within its own ranks. According to a recent report, the quickly-changing landscape of alternative investing strategies has seen a sudden rise in the prominence of artificial intelligence-based (AI) funds, and that many of these funds are vastly outperforming so-called "traditional quants", as well as human-led management teams.

Fascinated by the modern concepts of finance and my innate passion for mathematics , I kept reading and collecting nuances from many sources for my own understanding but then thought to share with my small world of friends, peers and audience... the story of fault line in modern finance: Invasion of AI in Quant world !

The dramatic change in the fortunes of 7.5 billion people has, not surprisingly, generated tremendous interest in the world economy post 2008-09 crisis. Pramod Singh offers the first major account of how this has come about and what more the worldwide leadership must do to sustain its rapid growth in the wake of Artificial Intelligence and its invasion in Modern Financial System. It will be must reading for everyone interested in modern financial system, its fault lines, global foreign affairs, or the world economy.

Author

Alumnus of IIT BHU Varanasi and IIM Calcutta, Pramod is an Indian Author. Wharton and Yale helped him grasp the nuances of Finance. Writing of Pramod gets the glimpses of the cultural diversity from the 5000 year old city called Kashi , his hometown, to the city of dreams, Mumbai, where he is based. His wife Dr Surabhi is PhD from IIT Dhanbad and blessed with two kids, Kuhoo & Keshoo.

www.ingramcontent.com/pod-product-compliance
Lightning Source LLC
Chambersburg PA
CBHW030942070326
40689CB00042B/1547